STARS OF SPORTS

A'JA WILSON
BASKETBALL SHOOTING STAR

by Matt Chandler

CAPSTONE PRESS
a capstone imprint

Published by Capstone Press, an imprint of Capstone
1710 Roe Crest Drive, North Mankato, Minnesota 56003
capstonepub.com

Copyright © 2026 by Capstone. All rights reserved. No part of this publication may be reproduced in whole or in part, or stored in a retrieval system, or transmitted in any form or by any means, electronic, mechanical, photocopying, recording, or otherwise, without written permission of the publisher.

SPORTS ILLUSTRATED KIDS is a trademark of ABG-SI LLC. Used with permission.

Library of Congress Cataloging-in-Publication Data is available on the Library of Congress website.
ISBN: 9798875222573 (hardcover)
ISBN: 9798875222528 (paperback)
ISBN: 9798875222535 (ebook PDF)

Summary: A'ja Wilson was on the varsity basketball team as a middle schooler, and she never slowed down. She played for the University of South Carolina and was drafted first overall by the Las Vegas Aces in 2018. Her hard work is evident in this encouraging sports biography.

Editorial Credits
Editor: Patrick Donnelly; Designer: Sarah Bennett; Media Researcher: Svetlana Zhurkin; Production Specialist: Tori Abraham

Image Credits
Associated Press: File/Julie Jacobson, 20, The Sun News/Janet Blackmon Morgan, 13; Getty Images: © 2018 NBAE/Ned Dishman, 21, © 2019 NBAE/Joe Murphy, 23, © 2022 NBAE/Brian Babineau, 25, © 2023 NBAE/Derek White, 5, Ethan Miller, cover, 7, 11, 22, 28, Fotokita, 1, Gregory Shamus, 19, Jonathan Daniel, 14, Kevin C. Cox, 9, Ron Jenkins, 16, 17, Sarah Stier, 27, Steph Chambers, 26; Newscom: MCT/The State/Tracy Glantz, 15

Source Notes
Page 6, 7, "So many people have been a part . . .", "I felt like it was . . ." Megan Santaniello, "Hometown Hopefuls: A'ja Wilson credits success to church and community, where her story is a beacon of hope." NBCSports.com, August 1, 2023, https://www.nbcsports.com/on-her-turf/news/hometown-hopefuls-aja-wilson-wnba-basketball-church-community-south-carolina. Accessed December 2024.

Page 8, 9, 10, "She wasn't as good . . .", "We got the good gym . . .", "I really want to play . . ." Katie Barnes, "WNBA playoffs give Las Vegas Aces' A'ja Wilson chance to cement her status as an icon." ESPN.com, October 8, 2021, https://www.espn.ph/wnba/story/_/id/32266763/wnba-playoffs-give-las-vegas-aces-aja-wilson-chance-cement-status-icon. Accessed December 2024.

Page 11, "If you can't stand up . . ." Sean Hurd, "Las Vegas Aces forward A'ja Wilson puts mother's lessons into book 'Dear Black Girls: How to Be True to You.'" andscape.com, February 6, 2024, https://andscape.com/features/las-vegas-aces-forward-aja-wilson-puts-mothers-lessons-into-book-dear-black-girls-how-to-be-true-to-you/. Accessed December 2024.

Page 12, "Dominant left-handed power forward . . ." "A'ja Wilson (recruiting page)." ESPN.com, https://insider.espn.com/college-sports/basketball/recruiting/player/evaluation/_/id/139025/aja-wilson. Accessed December 2024.

Page 15, "It was very tough . . ." "A'ja Wilson picks USC, discusses her decision (video)." The State, https://www.youtube.com/watch?v=5yp7MhFC2FE. Accessed December 2024.

Page 15, "It truly is . . ." Walter Villa, "A'ja Wilson chooses South Carolina." ESPN.com, April 16, 2024, https://www.espn.com/espnw/news-commentary/story/_/id/10790508/hoopgurlz-south-carolina-gamecocks-get-commitment-aja-wilson-no-1-prospect-espnw-hoopgurlz-top-100-2014-recruiting-class. Accessed December 2024.

Page 19, "I have had a great four years . . ." "A Look Back at A'ja Wilson's Gamecock Career." gamecocksonline.com, April 10, 2018, https://gamecocksonline.com/news/2018/04/10/a-look-back-at-a-ja-wilson-s-gamecock-career/. Accessed December 2024.

Page 20, "With the first pick . . ." "WNBA Draft 2018: All the results of the 1st round! (video)." WNBA, https://www.youtube.com/watch?v=FaZeEYi3NLg. Accessed December 2024.

Page 23, "Columbia's home." Jeremiah Holloway, "'Columbia's home': Gamecock great, WNBA star A'ja Wilson gives back to hometown." The State, November 14, 2022, https://www.thestate.com/sports/college/university-of-south-carolina/usc-womens-basketball/article268704857.html. Accessed December 2024.

Any additional websites and resources referenced in this book are not maintained, authorized, or sponsored by Capstone. All product and company names are trademarks™ or registered® trademarks of their respective holders.

Printed and bound in China.   006276

TABLE OF CONTENTS

SCORING MACHINE.. 4

CHAPTER ONE
SOUTHERN ROOTS 6

CHAPTER TWO
HIGH SCHOOL STAR.. 10

CHAPTER THREE
CLOSE TO HOME 14

CHAPTER FOUR
VIVA LAS VEGAS 20

CHAPTER FIVE
WNBA CHAMPION 24

TIMELINE...29

GLOSSARY..30

READ MORE..31

INTERNET SITES 31

INDEX 32

Words in **BOLD** are in the glossary.

SCORING MACHINE

On August 22, 2023, the Las Vegas Aces were in Atlanta to take on the Dream. A'ja Wilson was about to make history.

The Aces star started the game with a hot hand. She scored in the **paint**. She hit big shots from the outside. She drove the lane for buckets. By halftime, Wilson led her team with 22 points.

Her **domination** continued in the second half. With less than a minute to play, Wilson had scored 51 points. The WNBA record was 53. It looked like Wilson might fall short of the record. Then the unexpected happened. Atlanta coach Tanisha Wright was **ejected** from the game for arguing with the officials. The Aces were awarded two free throws. Wilson made both shots to end her historic run with a record-tying 53 points! Best of all, the Aces got the win, 112–100.

>>> A'ja Wilson shoots a free throw on her record-setting night against Atlanta.

CHAPTER ONE
SOUTHERN ROOTS

A'ja Riyadh Wilson was born on August 8, 1996, in Columbia, South Carolina. Her dad, Roscoe, played professional basketball in Europe. Her mom, Eva, was a court reporter. A'ja's brother, Renaldo, also played professional basketball.

Wilson grew up in Hopkins, South Carolina. She was surrounded by a large and loving family. She credits her parents, grandparents, aunts, and uncles for her success. "So many people have been a part of the village to help raise me," she said.

FACT

Wilson says she got her unique first name from her dad. His favorite song was "Aja" by the band Steely Dan.

Wilson is one of the hardest-working players in the WNBA. She traces that **discipline** back to her childhood. Wilson says she inherited her grandmother Hattie's drive. "I felt like it was always instilled in me," she said.

Wilson didn't want to play basketball when she was a child. She played tennis, soccer, and volleyball. She liked to swim. She took classes in karate, ballet, and tap dance.

》》 Wilson stands between her mother, Eva, and her father, Roscoe, after she was named the WNBA Most Valuable Player (MVP) in 2024.

A LOVE OF THE GAME

Wilson's dad never gave up on his dream that his daughter would follow in his footsteps and play basketball. Finally, when Wilson was 11 years old, her dad used a **bribe** to get his daughter to give basketball a try. He bought her a new pair of basketball shoes before tryouts for a team he wanted her to join.

The bribe worked. Wilson went to the tryout and made the team. However, she was not a good basketball player at first. Wilson says her main role on her first team was to get water and cheer on her teammates. Her dad coached the team along with Jerome Dickerson. "She wasn't as good as the other girls," Dickerson said. "She was just there."

Wilson's dad took her to a basketball camp run by University of South Carolina coach Dawn Staley. The coaches at camp divided players up by their skill level.

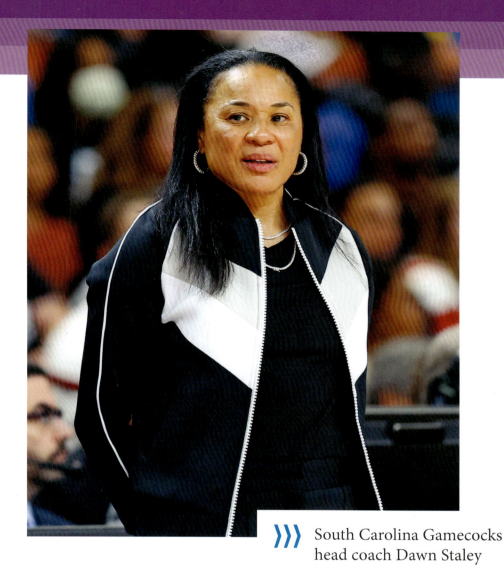

››› South Carolina Gamecocks head coach Dawn Staley

"We got the good gym, we got the OK gym, and we got the bad gym," Staley recalled. "A'ja qualified for the bad gym."

Still, Roscoe Wilson never gave up on his daughter. Soon her natural athletic ability began to take over.

CHAPTER TWO
HIGH SCHOOL STAR

Wilson loved being on the team, but watching from the bench grew old.

"I really want to play," she recalled saying at the time. She knew that getting a chance to play in the games would make her really happy.

Wilson began to work harder. She practiced at home. She came to practice early and left late. And by the time she reached eighth grade, Wilson had become an excellent basketball player.

Wilson attended Heathwood Hall Episcopal School in Columbia. In eighth grade, she earned a spot on the varsity team. Playing with girls up to four years older, Wilson still flashed her skills. She averaged 14 points and eight rebounds per game in her first season.

>>> Wilson and her mom celebrate on the court after an Aces victory in 2024.

Messages from Mom

Wilson is known as a tough competitor on the basketball court. She doesn't back down from a challenge or an opponent. It's one of many life lessons she learned from her mom. Eva Wilson taught her daughter to always stand up for herself. Her mom's advice was simple: "If you can't stand up for yourself, call me. I will."

Today, Wilson calls her mom her best friend. The two are also business partners. They launched Burnt Wax Candles, a business Eva runs. It combines two of Wilson's biggest passions—her lifelong love of candles and her love for her mom.

SOMETHING SPECIAL

Wilson continued to grow and develop at Heathwood Hall. As a freshman, she appeared in 25 games. She averaged 22 points and 15.4 rebounds per game. But her talents were not limited to basketball. Wilson earned all-state honors in volleyball.

College scouts began watching Wilson's games. They were there when she led the Highlanders to the state semifinals in 2012. They took note when she carried the team to second place in the state tournament in 2013. And, in 2014, when Heathwood Hall won the Class 3A South Carolina state championship, Wilson was the top-ranked player in the nation. The scouting report on Wilson summed up her impact as a player.

"Dominant left-handed power forward with size to impact both on the block and on the **perimeter**," the report said. "Next-level impact."

FACT

During high school, Wilson was diagnosed with **dyslexia**. Today, she uses her experiences to support others who live with the learning disability.

Wilson drives to the basket for Heathwood Hall in December 2013.

CHAPTER THREE
CLOSE TO HOME

In her senior year, Wilson was the top girl's high school player in the country. She averaged 34.4 points per game in the Highlanders' championship season. She had offers to play at some of the biggest colleges in the United States. Tennessee, North Carolina, South Carolina, and Connecticut all wanted Wilson.

》》》 Wilson looks for room to dribble in the 2014 McDonald's All-American Game.

>>> A relieved and happy Wilson announces her college decision on April 16, 2014.

The Heathwood Hall gymnasium was packed on April 16, 2014. They were there to hear Wilson announce her college decision. She decided to stay close to home and play for the South Carolina Gamecocks.

"It was very tough, because it was just four great programs," she said at the press conference announcing her decision.

Coach Staley said, "It truly is a great day to be a Gamecock."

FACT

Wilson received so many recruiting letters, they filled four bins. Her parents kept them as a part of their daughter's legacy.

HEART OF A CHAMPION

The American Airlines Center was rocking on April 2, 2017. More than 19,000 fans packed the arena in Dallas, Texas. They were there to watch Wilson's top-ranked Gamecocks take on No. 2 Mississippi State for the NCAA National Championship.

It was the end of a brilliant season for Wilson. In 35 games, the junior averaged nearly 18 points and eight rebounds and led the team with 90 blocked shots. Could she help them hold off Mississippi State?

Wilson scored early and often. She beat double teams. She drove to the basket. She made her free throws. And, when it mattered most, Wilson delivered. Late in the fourth quarter, South Carolina led 62–52. If the Bulldogs were to pull off a comeback, they needed to shut down Wilson. Instead, she finished them off.

>>> Mississippi State's Teaira McCowan can't get past Wilson in the 2017 National Championship game.

First, Wilson had a huge block to get the ball back. On the other end, Tyasha Harris fed Wilson a quick pass inside. The junior split two defenders and banked a shot off the glass. The Gamecocks defeated Mississippi State 67–55. Wilson was a national champion!

FACT

Wilson finished the national championship game with 23 points and 10 rebounds.

>>> The Gamecocks celebrate after winning the national title.

READY TO GO PRO

The Gamecocks returned to the NCAA Tournament in Wilson's senior year. But they could not capture the magic of 2017. Their March Madness run ended in the Elite 8 with a loss to Connecticut.

Though her senior season ended in disappointment, Wilson's college career ranks among the best ever. She left South Carolina holding 86 school records. She is the Gamecocks' all-time scoring leader with 2,389 points. The 6-foot-4 (193-centimeter) superstar also set the school record with 363 blocked shots!

The four-time **All-American** led her team to a national title. She won countless individual honors. Now it was time to take her talents to the professional stage.

"I have had a great four years," Wilson said after her final college game. "Coming to South Carolina was *the* best decision I've made."

FACT

In 2021, the University of South Carolina unveiled an 11-foot-(3-meter) tall bronze statue of Wilson outside its basketball arena.

››› Wilson shows off her gold medal at the 2020 Olympics.

Olympic Gold Medalist

Wilson was named to the U.S. national team for the 2020 Olympics. She started all six Olympic games for Team USA. She averaged more than 16 points and seven rebounds per game. Her strong play helped lead the United States to the gold medal!

19

CHAPTER FOUR
VIVA LAS VEGAS

"With the first pick in the 2018 WNBA Draft, the Las Vegas Aces select A'ja Wilson." With that announcement by WNBA president Lisa Borders, Wilson's dream had come true.

Wilson made her WNBA **debut** against the Connecticut Sun. The rookie seemed a bit nervous. She missed her first four shots and turned the ball over early. But midway through the first quarter, center Kelsey Bone scooped up a loose ball. She passed it to Wilson. The rookie banked it off the glass for the first points of her professional career. She finished her first WNBA game with 14 points and 10 rebounds.

》》》 WNBA president Lisa Borders greets Wilson after announcing the former Gamecocks star as the first pick of the 2018 draft.

The Aces struggled in 2018 and missed the playoffs. But Wilson had an immediate impact. She earned a trip to the All-Star Game. She was named the WNBA Rookie of the Year. She played in 33 of the team's 34 games and led the Aces in scoring, rebounds, and blocks per game.

》》》 Wilson was given her WNBA Rookie of the Year Award during halftime of a Team USA exhibition game in September 2018.

21

BETTER THAN EVER

Many players suffer a so-called sophomore slump. But Wilson's second WNBA season saw her become one of the bright young superstars of the league.

Wilson played a huge role in the Aces turning around their fortunes. She earned her second trip to the All-Star Game. The team went 21–13 in the regular season. And they reached the playoffs.

Las Vegas hosted the Chicago Sky in a winner-take-all game to advance to the semifinals. Wilson played a supporting role. Her 11 points and 11 rebounds contributed to a 93–92 victory.

The Aces were eliminated in the next round. But Wilson had gotten a taste of the playoffs, and she wanted more.

》》》 Wilson looks for space as Los Angeles Sparks defenders Chelsea Gray and Chiney Ogwumike close in.

>>> Wilson talks to a group of young girls at a basketball camp in 2019.

Giving Back

Wilson is one of many pro athletes who give their time and money to support their communities. In 2019, she launched the A'ja Wilson Foundation. The group works to stop bullying in schools. She also focuses on children living with dyslexia. She donates school supplies for children in need. She raises money for scholarships. And she never forgets her South Carolina roots.

"Columbia's home. It's where my heart will always be," Wilson said. "To come back and give back to the community is something that I take a lot of pride in because it's raised me."

CHAPTER FIVE
WNBA CHAMPION

After four years in the league, Wilson had done everything but win a championship. Would 2022 be her season?

Wilson and the Aces started red-hot. The team won nine of its first 10 games. Las Vegas finished the regular season 26–10, the best record in the Western Conference. Wilson was a force on defense. She led the team with 1.9 blocks and 9.4 rebounds per game.

In the playoffs, Wilson didn't let up. She averaged more than 20 points and 10 rebounds per game. It all came down to Game 4 of the WNBA Finals. Las Vegas had beaten Connecticut in two of the first three games. A win on the road would give the Aces their first title.

Wilson struggled offensively all night. She made just four of her 13 shots from the floor. But she grabbed 14 rebounds and had two blocks and two steals. The Aces knocked off the Sun 78–71 to capture the WNBA title.

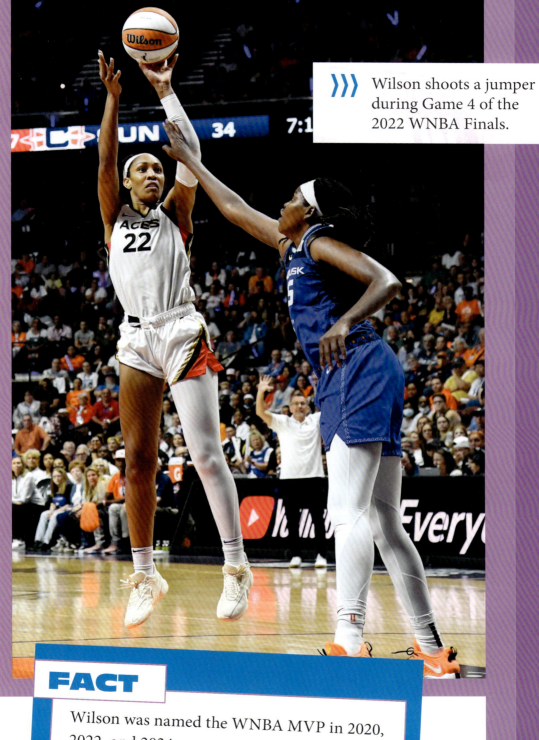

》》》 Wilson shoots a jumper during Game 4 of the 2022 WNBA Finals.

FACT

Wilson was named the WNBA MVP in 2020, 2022, and 2024.

25

>>> Wilson grabs a rebound in a May 2023 game against the Seattle Storm.

BACK-TO-BACK

Repeating as champions is one of the toughest things to do in sports. Wilson and her teammates planned to do just that in 2023. The Aces went 34–6, the best record in the league. Wilson had another great season on both sides of the ball. She averaged 22.8 points, 9.5 rebounds, and 2.2 blocks per game. But Wilson wanted more than big stats. She wanted another WNBA championship trophy.

The Aces once again returned to the finals. Wilson found herself in another Game 4, leading two games to one and ready to close out the title. Wilson took over and dominated the New York Liberty. She set the tone early, driving to the basket and muscling through the defense for the first points of the game. She never let up. In a battle that went down to the final shot, the Aces outlasted the Liberty 70–69 to win back-to-back WNBA championships!

It was a game of **redemption** for Wilson. She finished the game with 24 points and added 16 rebounds to help close out the Liberty.

》》》 Wilson and her teammates celebrate winning back-to-back WNBA titles.

》》》 Wilson holds her WNBA MVP trophy in September 2024.

2024 AND BEYOND

Wilson already has Hall of Fame **credentials**. She has won three league MVP awards. She has led her team to two WNBA championships. Wilson won her second Olympic gold medal in 2024. And she became the first player in WNBA history to score 1,000 points in a season. She finished 2024 with a career scoring average of 21.1 points per game. That is the best in WNBA history.

But Wilson is still in her prime. She wants more. The WNBA is filled with young superstars. But for now, no player has accomplished more than A'ja Wilson.

TIMELINE

1996 A'ja Wilson is born August 8 in Columbia, South Carolina.

2014 Wilson wins the South Carolina State Basketball Championship as a member of the Heathwood Hall Episcopal School.

2015 Wilson accepts a basketball scholarship offer from the University of South Carolina Gamecocks.

2017 South Carolina wins the National Championship, and Wilson is named Most Outstanding Player of the tournament.

2018 Wilson is drafted by the Las Vegas Aces with the No. 1 pick.

2020 Wilson wins her first WNBA MVP Award.

2021 Wilson wins her first Olympic gold medal with Team USA.

2022 Wilson is named WNBA MVP again and leads the Aces to their first league title.

2023 Wilson leads Las Vegas to another WNBA championship and is named Finals MVP.

2024 Wilson wins her second Olympic gold medal with Team USA.

2024 Wins her third WNBA MVP Award as the Aces fall short of a three-peat.

GLOSSARY

ALL-AMERICAN (AWL uh-MARE-ick-uhn)—an award or distinction given to the best players in the country

BRIBE (BRYB)—money or other goods given in an attempt to convince another to do something

CREDENTIALS (cre-DEN-chulz)—qualifications or qualities of success

DEBUT (day-BEW)—first appearance

DISCIPLINE (DIS-uh-plin)—self-control

DOMINATION (dom-eh-NAY-shun)—total control

DYSLEXIA (dis-LEX-ee-ya)—a learning disorder that affects the ability to read or write

EJECTED (ee-JEK-tuhd)—thrown out of a game

PAINT (PAYNT)—in basketball, the area from the end line to the free throw line in front of the basket; also known as the lane

PERIMETER (pur-RIM-eh-ter)—the outside edge

REDEMPTION (re-DEM-chun)—making up for a previous error or defeat

READ MORE

Chandler, Matt. *Caitlin Clark: Basketball Phenom.* North Mankato, MN: Capstone, 2025.

Flynn, Brendan. *Basketball Records Smashed!* North Mankato, MN: Capstone, 2024.

Kjartansson, Kjartan. *Legends of the NBA.* New York: Abbeville Press, 2022.

INTERNET SITES

A'ja Wilson Foundation
ajawilsonfoundation.org

Las Vegas Aces
aces.wnba.com

WNBA
wnba.com

INDEX

A'ja Wilson Foundation, 23
All-Star Game, 21, 22

Columbia, South Carolina, 6, 10, 23, 29

Heathwood Hall Episcopal School's Highlanders, 10, 12, 13, 14, 15, 29

Las Vegas Aces, 4, 11, 20, 21, 22, 24, 26, 27, 29

March Madness, 18
McDonald's All-American Game, 14
Most Valuable Player (MVP), 7, 25, 28, 29

NCAA National Championship, 16, 17, 18

Olympic Games, 19, 28, 29

playoffs, 21, 22, 24

Staley, Dawn, 8, 9, 15

University of South Carolina Gamecocks, 9, 15, 16, 17, 18, 20, 29

Wilson, Roscoe, 6, 7, 8, 9
WNBA Rookie of the Year, 21

AUTHOR BIO

Matt Chandler is the author of more than 60 books for children and thousands of articles published in newspapers and magazines. He writes mostly nonfiction books with a focus on sports, ghosts and haunted places, and graphic novels. Matt lives in New York.